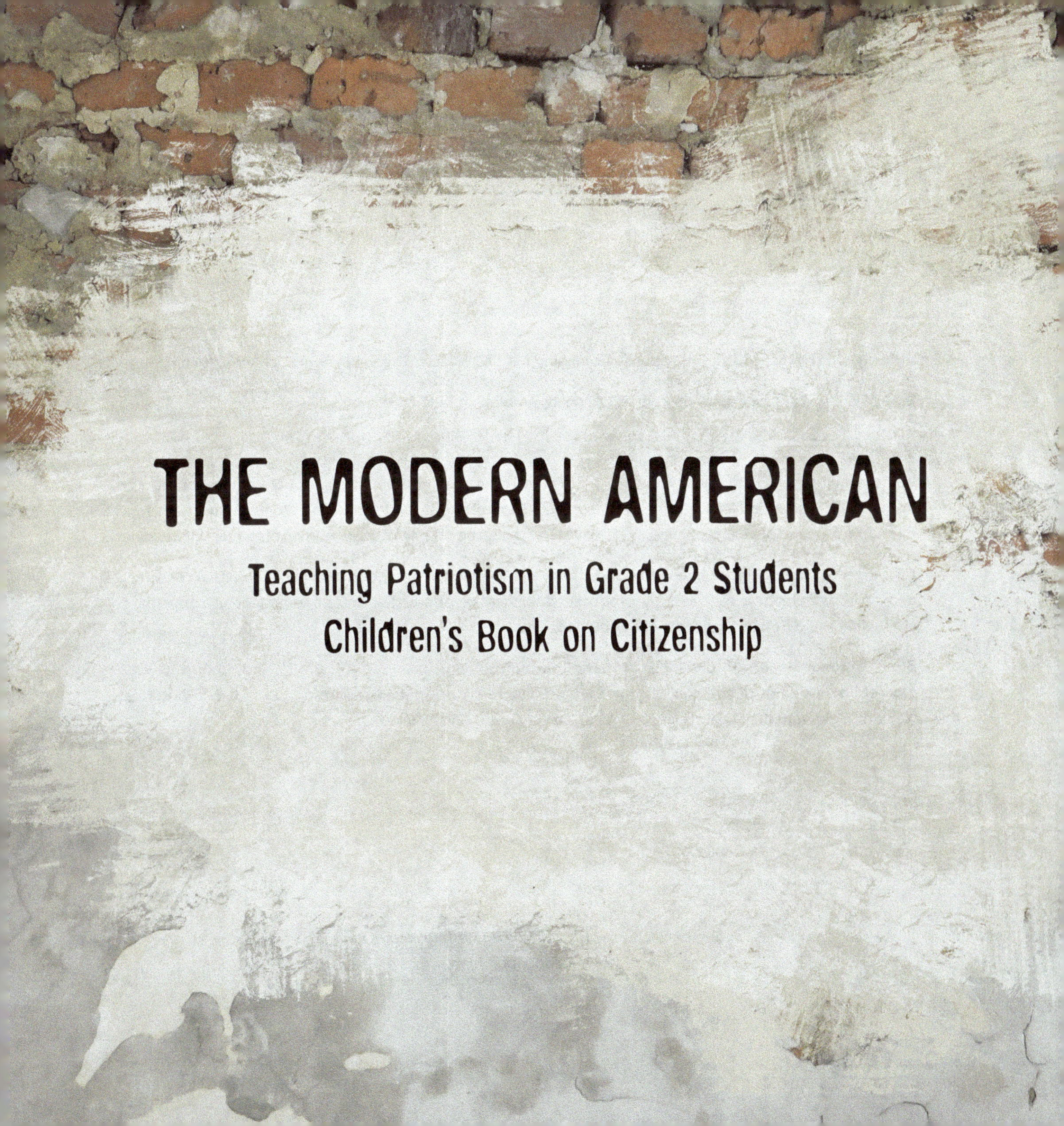

THE MODERN AMERICAN

Teaching Patriotism in Grade 2 Students
Children's Book on Citizenship

First Edition, 2024

Published in the United States by Speedy Publishing LLC, 40 E Main Street, Newark, Delaware 19711 USA.

Baby Professor Books are available at special discounts when purchased in bulk for industrial and sales-promotional use. For details contact our Special Sales Team at Speedy Publishing LLC, 40 E Main Street, Newark, Delaware 19711 USA. Telephone (888) 248-4521 Fax: (210) 519-4043.

10 9 8 7 6 * 5 4 3 2 1

Print Edition: 9781541987500
Digital Edition: 9781541987890
Hardcover Edition: 9781541989979

See the world in pictures. Build your knowledge in style.
www.speedypublishing.com

TABLE OF CONTENTS

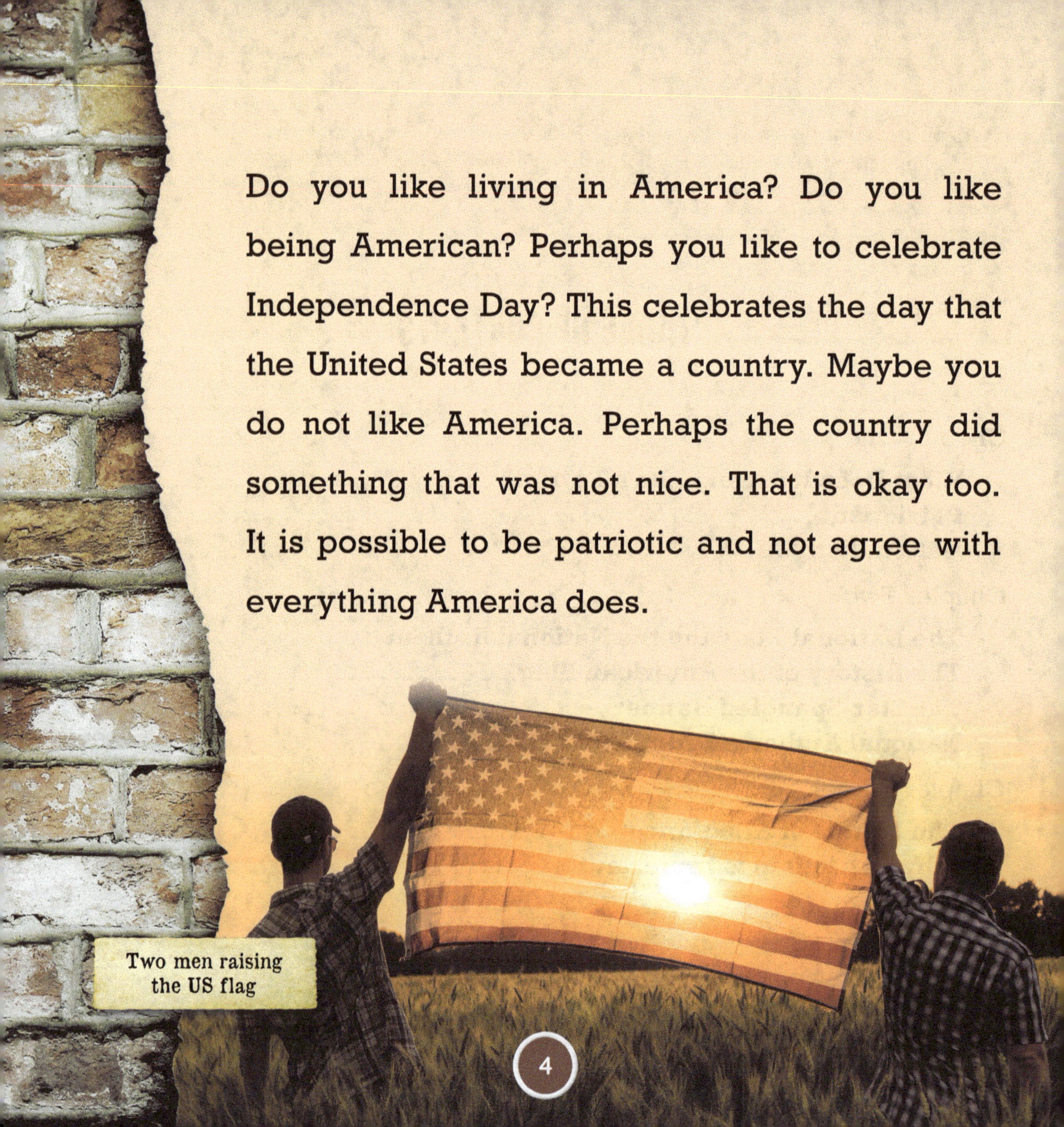

Do you like living in America? Do you like being American? Perhaps you like to celebrate Independence Day? This celebrates the day that the United States became a country. Maybe you do not like America. Perhaps the country did something that was not nice. That is okay too. It is possible to be patriotic and not agree with everything America does.

Two men raising the US flag

Americans have the freedom to disagree. This is an important right that the first Americans fought for. It is a freedom not everyone has. That is why we need to honor it and keep trying to make America a great place to live. This book will teach all about what it means to be patriotic. It will teach about the national flag, the anthem, and the pledge of allegiance.

Americans have the
freedom to disagree.

What Does it Mean to be a Patriot?

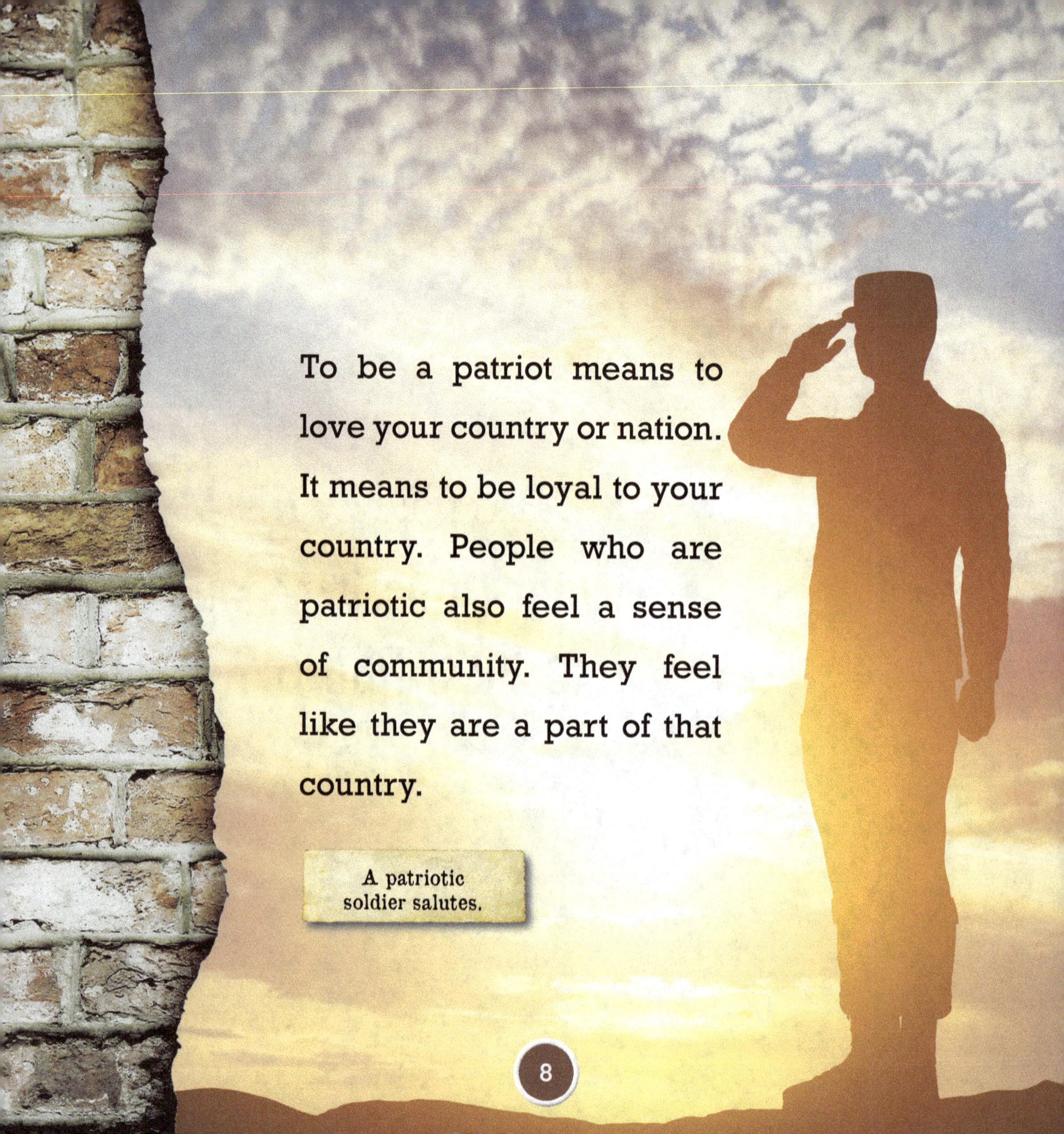

To be a patriot means to love your country or nation. It means to be loyal to your country. People who are patriotic also feel a sense of community. They feel like they are a part of that country.

A patriotic soldier salutes.

Patriotism

Patriotism can be a good thing. It brings people together. People from the same country feel loyal to each other. It provides a sense of community. Patriots also want to support their country. They want their country to be good.

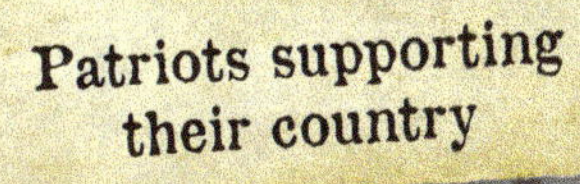
Patriots supporting their country

Being patriotic does not mean always agreeing. You can think your country does bad things sometimes. When this happens, patriotic people want to improve their country.

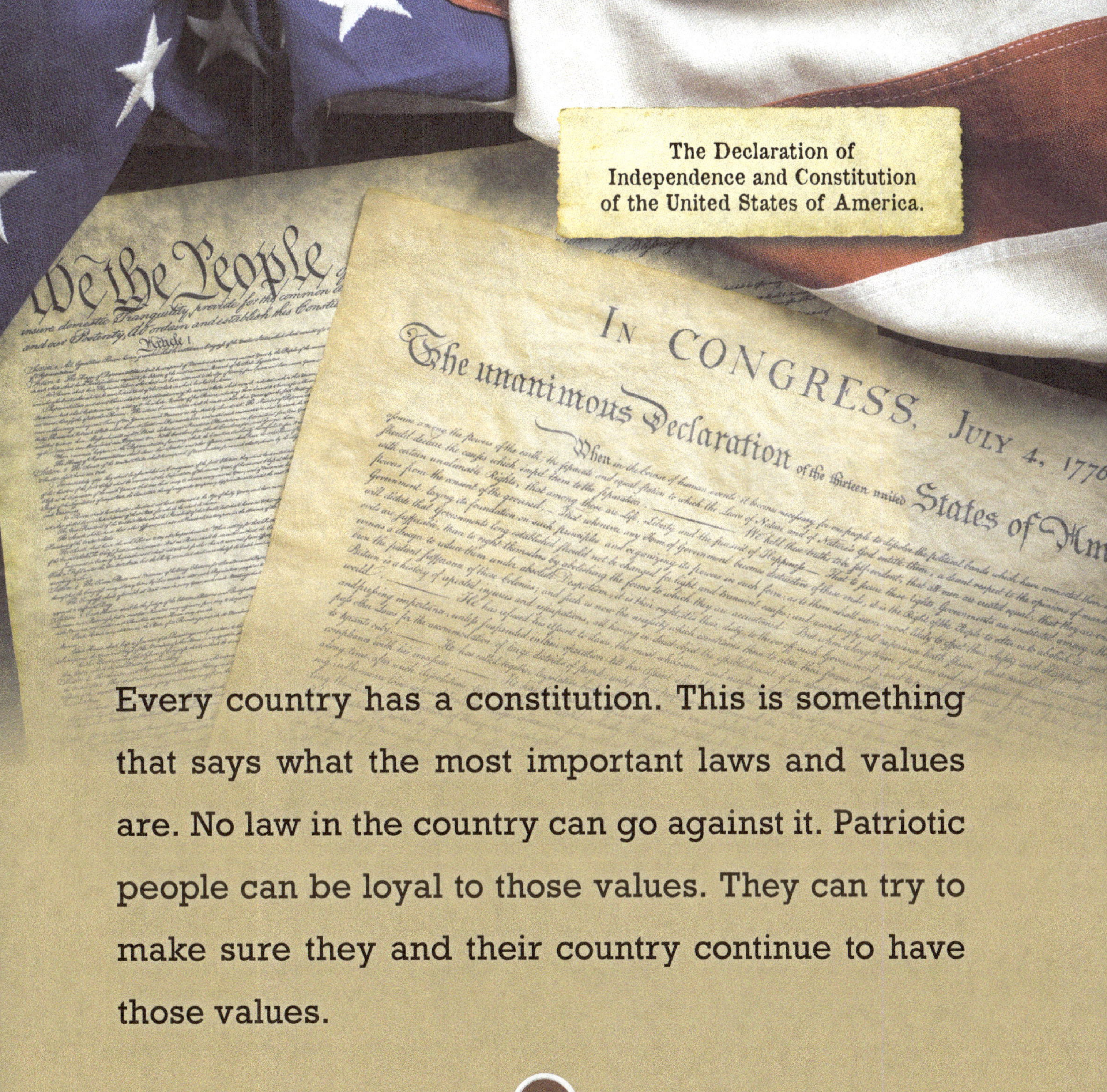

Every country has a constitution. This is something that says what the most important laws and values are. No law in the country can go against it. Patriotic people can be loyal to those values. They can try to make sure they and their country continue to have those values.

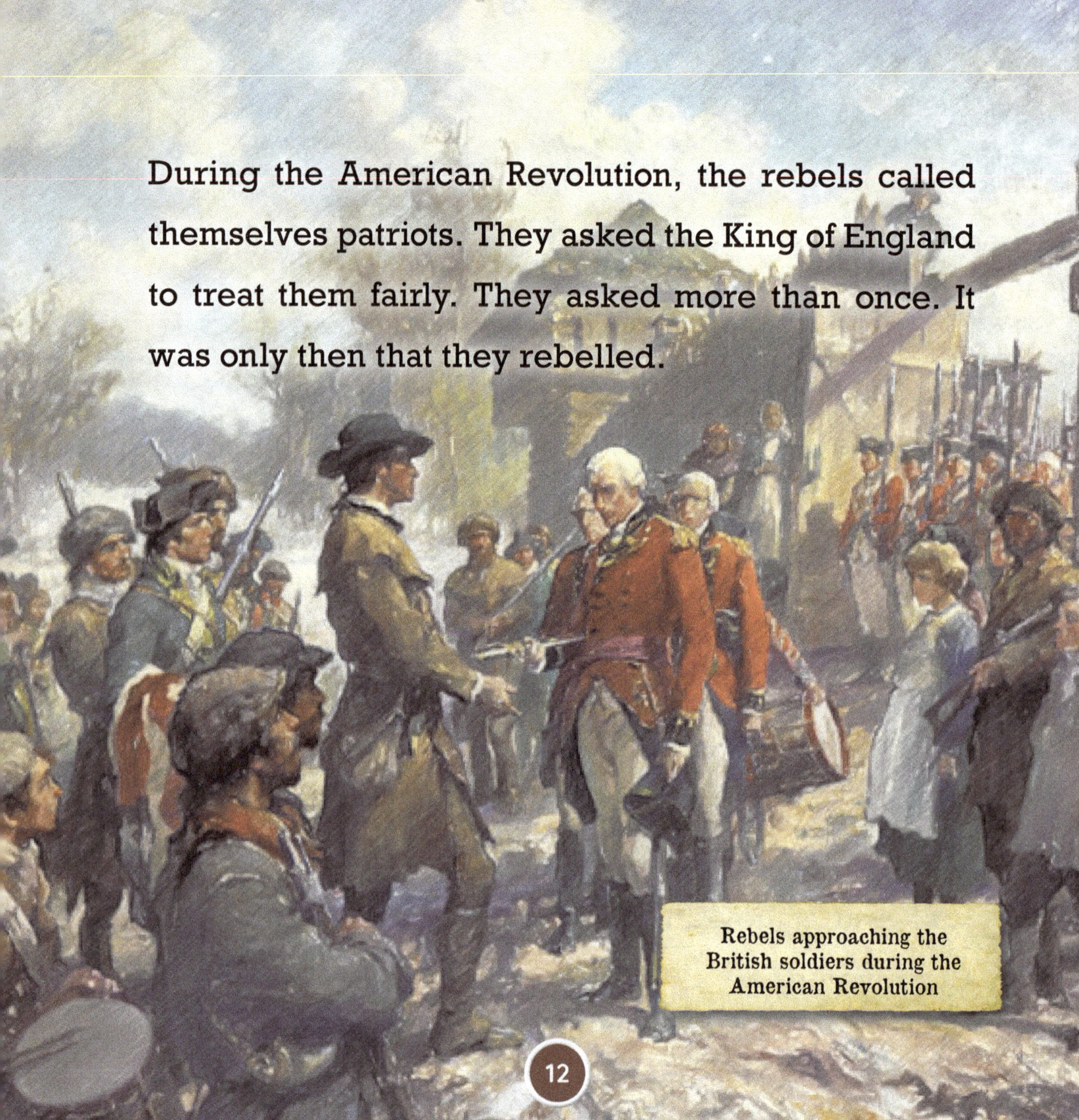

During the American Revolution, the rebels called themselves patriots. They asked the King of England to treat them fairly. They asked more than once. It was only then that they rebelled.

Rebels approaching the British soldiers during the American Revolution

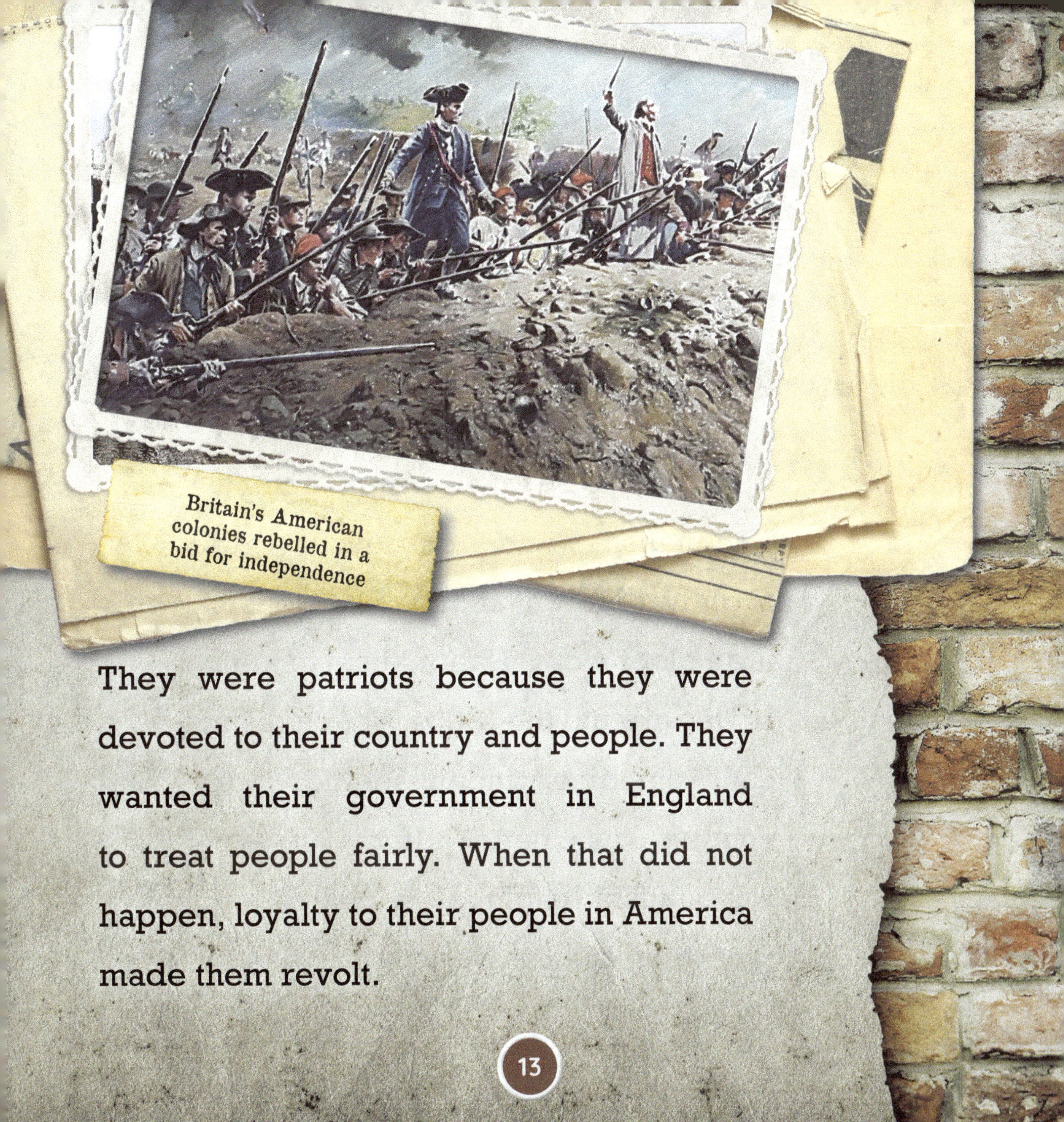

They were patriots because they were devoted to their country and people. They wanted their government in England to treat people fairly. When that did not happen, loyalty to their people in America made them revolt.

Nationalism

Nationalism and patriotism are sometimes used the same way. They both mean to be loyal to your country. Nationalism and patriotism are slightly different though. Patriotism is an older word. Nationalism though began around the 1800s. Nationalism can sometimes mean seeing your country as better than others. Nationalism might also make you ignore problems your country has.

National flags of
various countries

15

Many people think that nationalism helped lead to World War I. Many people felt their country was the best. They also took pride in all being a certain type of people.

German infantry advancing during World War I

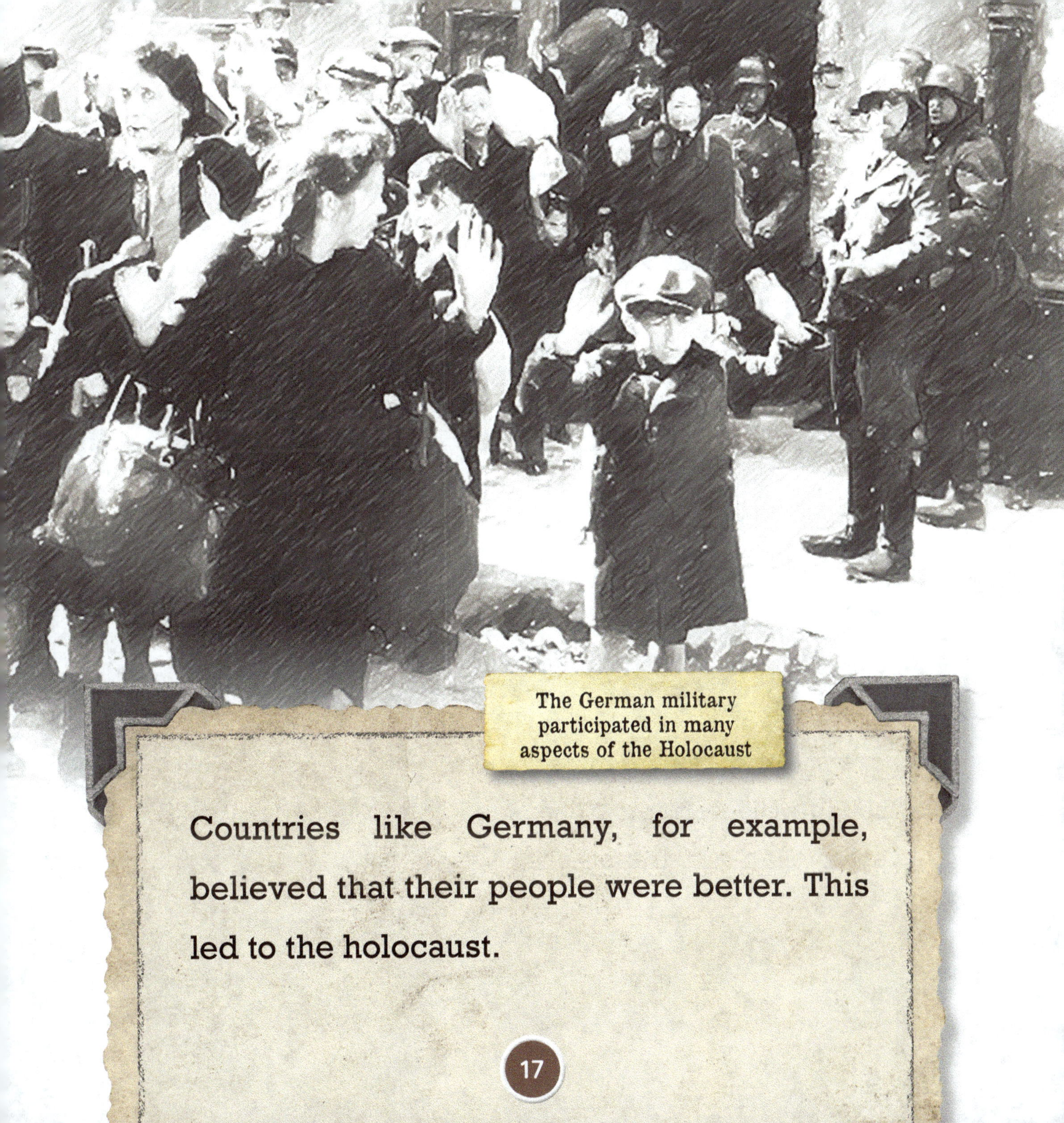

Countries like Germany, for example, believed that their people were better. This led to the holocaust.

DID YOU KNOW?

The holocaus what we call the killing of Jews during World War II in Germany. The Jews were brought to concentration camps. They could not leave. Millions of Jews were killed there. Hitler, Germany's leader, said the Jews were the problem in society. He thought the Germans race was better than all the others.

"Selection" of Hungarian Jews
on the ramp at Auschwitz
II-Birkenau in German

Adolf Hitler

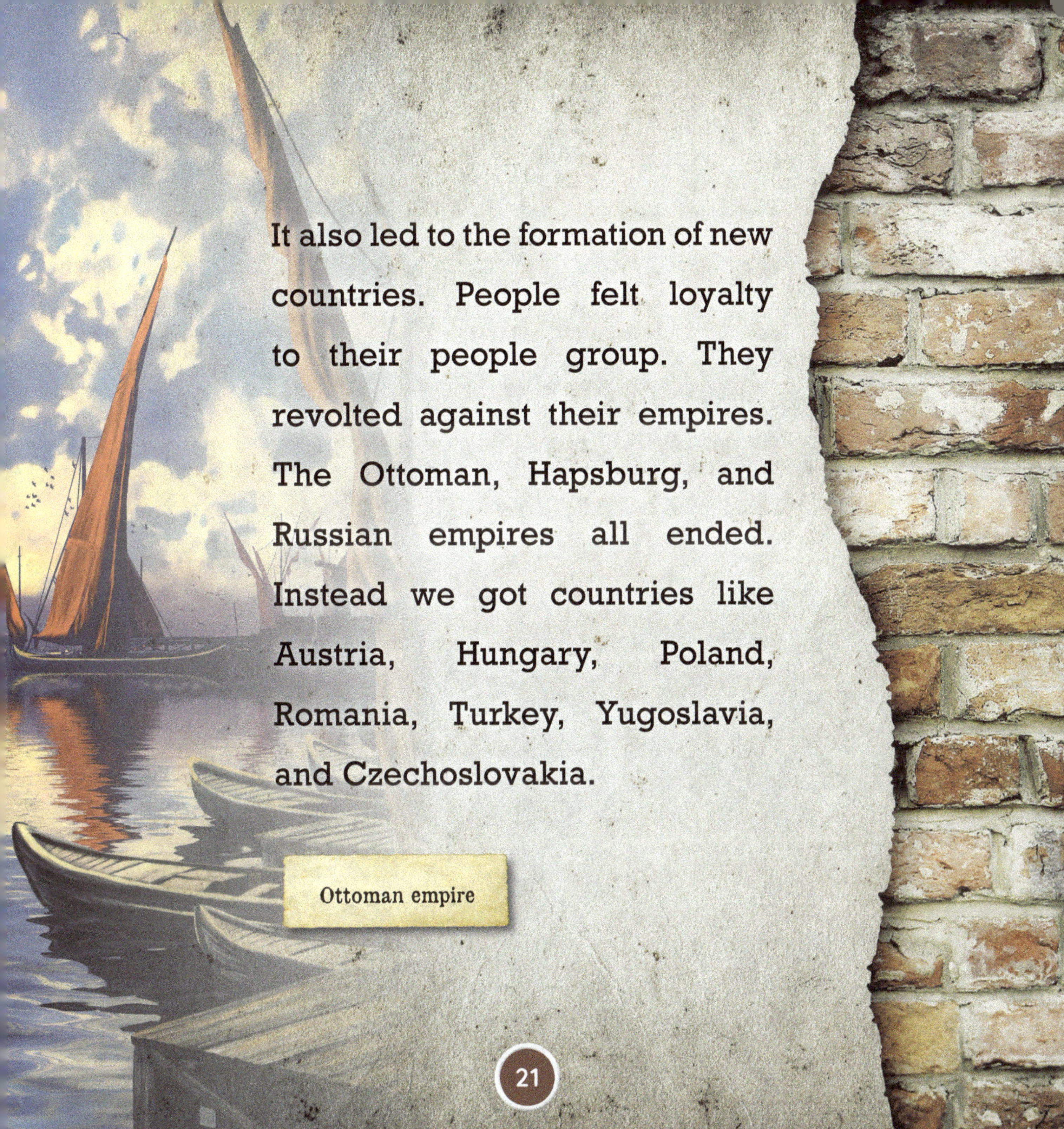

It also led to the formation of new countries. People felt loyalty to their people group. They revolted against their empires. The Ottoman, Hapsburg, and Russian empires all ended. Instead we got countries like Austria, Hungary, Poland, Romania, Turkey, Yugoslavia, and Czechoslovakia.

CHAPTER TWO

The National Flag and
the National Anthem

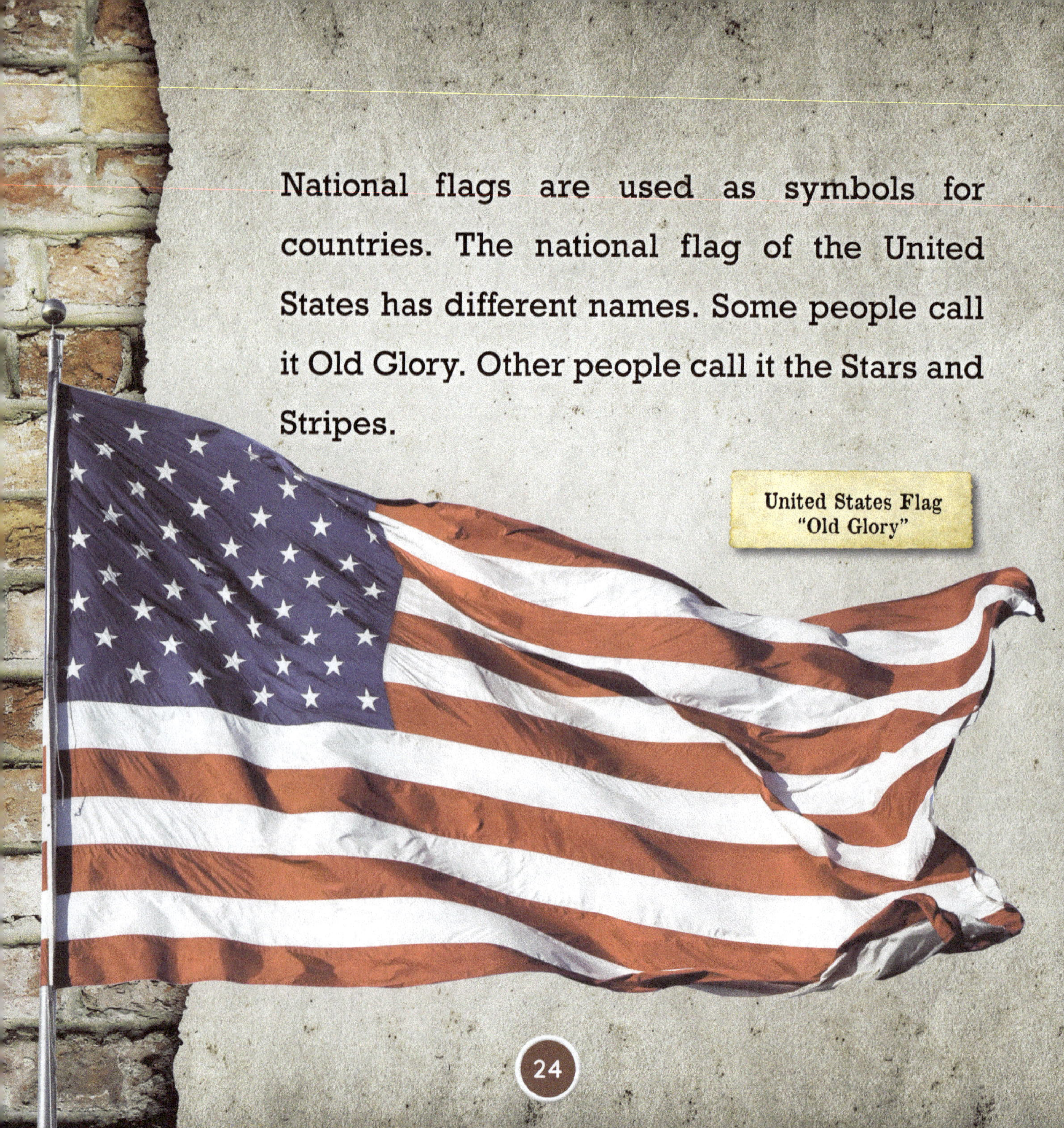

National flags are used as symbols for countries. The national flag of the United States has different names. Some people call it Old Glory. Other people call it the Stars and Stripes.

The Star spangled banner.

O say! can you see by the dawn's early light
What so proudly we hail'd at the twilight's last gleaming
Whose broad stripes and bright stars, through the clouds of the fight.
O'er the ramparts we watch'd were so gallantly streaming?

And the rocket's red glare – the bomb bursting in air
Gave proof through the night that our flag was still there?

O say, does that star-spangled banner yet wave
O'er the land of the free & the home of the brave?

Countries also have national anthems. This is a song people sing out of loyalty to their country. In the United States, the song is "The Star-Spangled Banner".

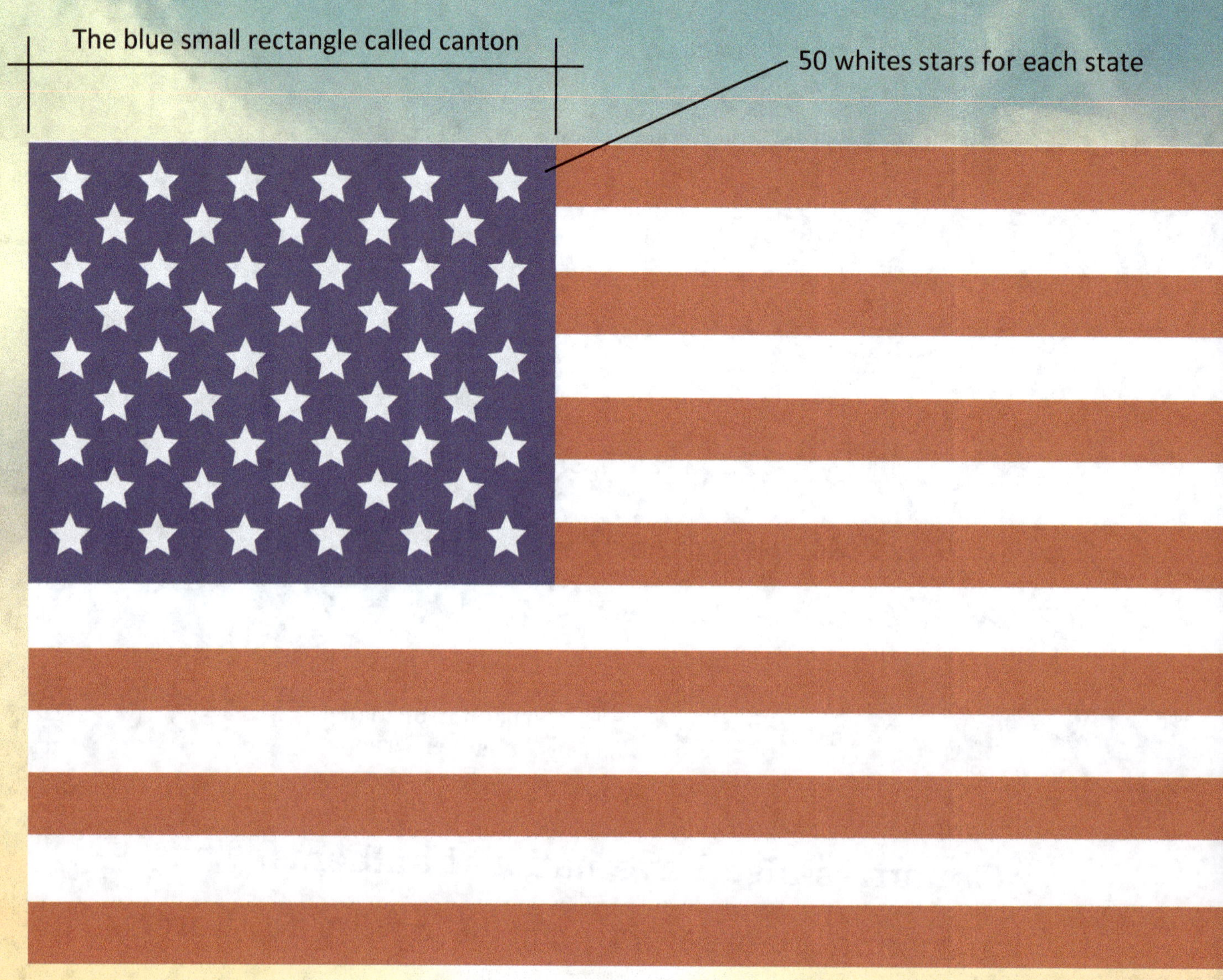

The American flag

The History of the American Flag

The American flag has white stars. These stars are on a small rectangle. This rectangle is found at the top right corner. This is called a canton. The American flag also has red and white stripes. These stripes go straight across.

Today, there are 50 white stars. These stars are for each state. There are also 13 stripes. Seven are red. Six are white. These are for the original American colonies. The flag has looked like this since 1960.

Thirteen stripes represents the original American colonies

The flag was different before 1960. It changed as different states joined the United States of America. With each new state, a new star and stripe would be added. In 1818, Congress decided the number of stripes would be thirteen. This would not change. The stars would change though to reflect the number of states.

BRANCHES OF GOVERNMENT

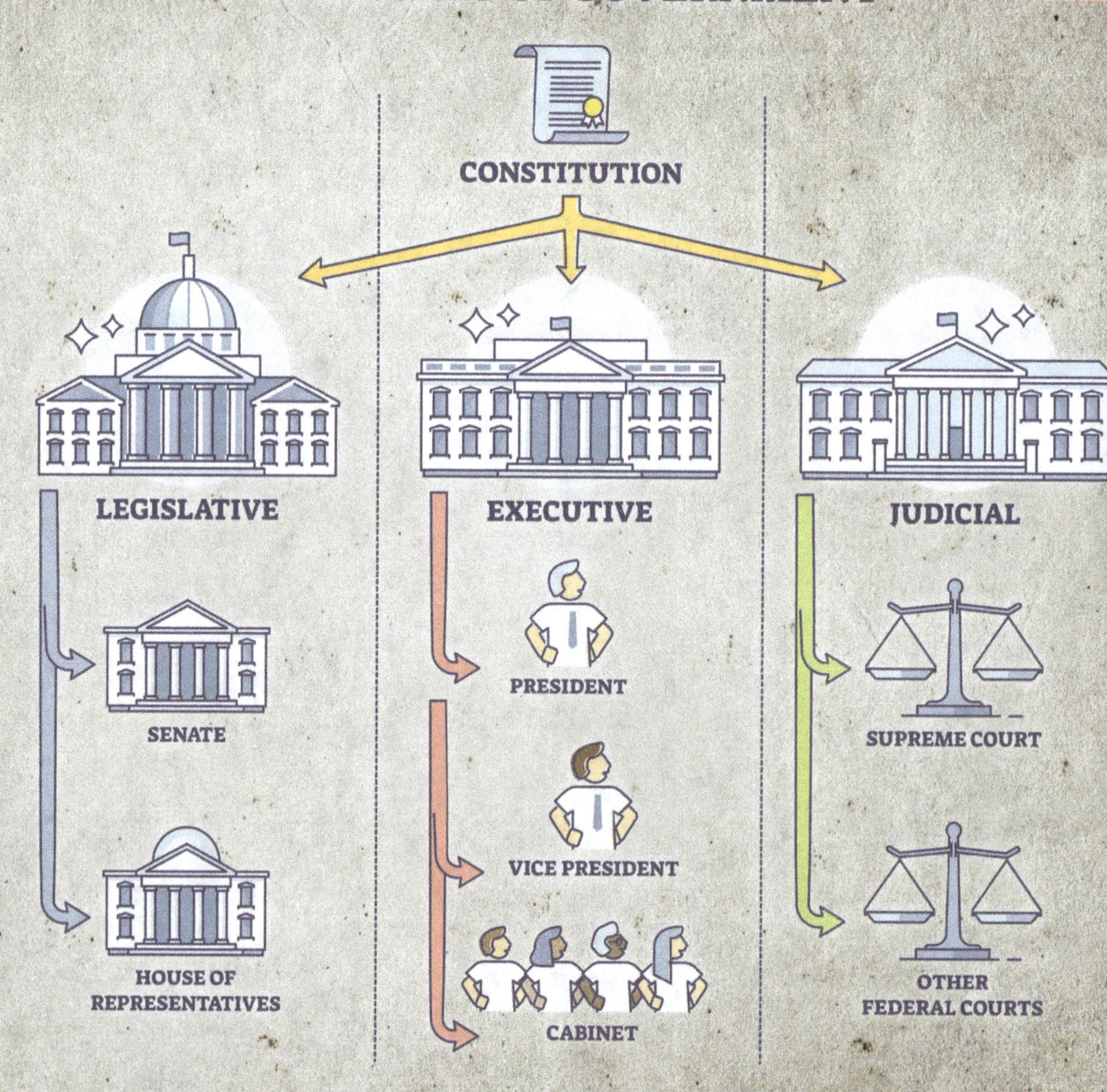

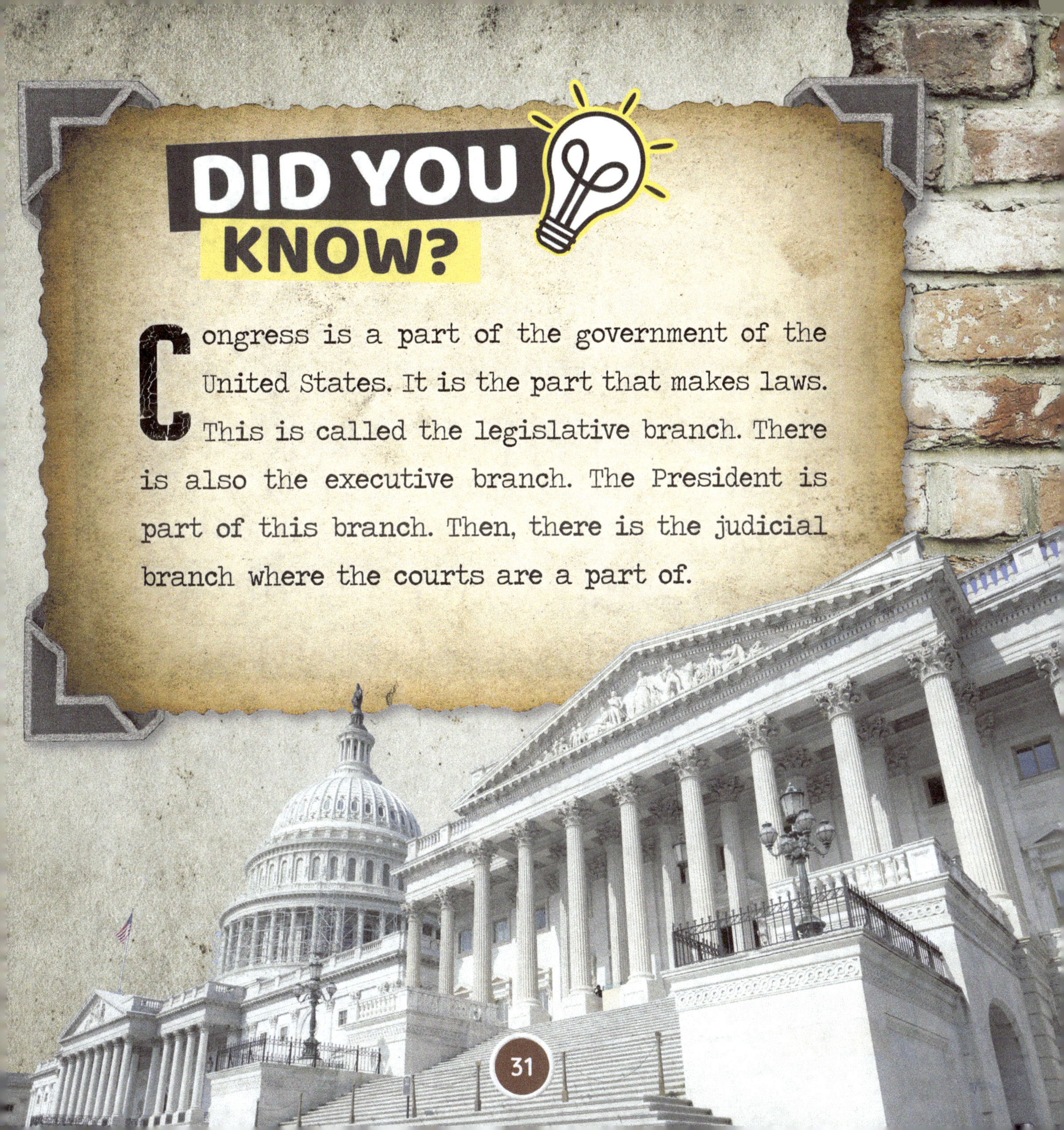

Congress is a part of the government of the United States. It is the part that makes laws. This is called the legislative branch. There is also the executive branch. The President is part of this branch. Then, there is the judicial branch where the courts are a part of.

The first official national flag was said to be made by Betsy Ross. No one knows for sure if that is true. Continental Congress approved the first national flag on June 14, 1777. This was after the American Revolutionary War had begun.

General George Washington seated on the left with Robert Morris, and standing, the Honorable George Ross, and with Betsy Ross seated on the right holding "The Nation's Flag."

The American Revolutionary War began in 1775. It lasted until 1783. That was almost ten years! The fighting ended in North America in 1781 though. It just took a while for a treaty to be formed and accepted. This was called the Treaty of Paris. A treaty is an agreement between two countries.

The American Revolutionary War

From left to right: John Jay, John Adams, Benjamin Franklin, Henry Laurens, and William Temple Franklin.

First and last pages of the Treaty of Paris

The Star-Spangled Banner

"The Star-Spangled Banner" was written by Francis Scott Key. He saw the flag waving after a victory. This was during the War of 1812. It was between the United States and Britain. The battle Scott saw was at Fort McHenry. It defended Baltimore, Maryland.

Battle at Fort
McHenry, 1814.
Francis Scott Key

Francis Scott Key with right arm stretched
out toward the United States and Dr.
William Beanes spy the American flag
waving above Baltimore's Fort Mc Henry.

Key was there because a friend of Key's was captured. His name was William Beanes. Since Key was a lawyer, he went to try and help negotiate for his friend's freedom. The British agreed. There was a condition though. Beanes and Key had to stay on their ship for the night.

During the night, the British attacked the fort. Key watched the battle happen. When dawn came, the flag was still flying! The British were not able to win.

The American flag was still flying after the Battle at Fort McHenry.

DEFENCE OF FORT M'HENRY.

The annexed song was composed under the following circumstances—A gentleman had left Baltimore, in a flag of truce for the purpose of getting released from the British fleet, a friend of his who had been captured at Marlborough.—He went as far as the mouth of the Patuxent, and was not permitted to return lest the intended attack on Baltimore should be disclosed. He was therefore brought up the Bay to the mouth of the Patapsco, where the flag vessel was kept under the guns of a frigate, and he was compelled to witness the bombardment of Fort M'Henry, which the Admiral had boasted that he would carry in a few hours, and that the city must fall. He watched the flag at the Fort through the whole day with an anxiety that can be better felt than described, until the night prevented him from seeing it. In the night he watched the Bomb Shells, and at early dawn his eye was again greeted by the proudly waving flag of his country.

Tune—ANACREON IN HEAVEN.

O! say can you see by the dawn's early light,
What so proudly we hailed at the twilight's last gleaming,
Whose broad stripes and bright stars through the perilous fight,
O'er the ramparts we watch'd, were so gallantly streaming?
And the Rockets' red glare, the Bombs bursting in air,
Gave proof through the night that our Flag was still there;

O! say does that star-spangled Banner yet wave,
O'er the Land of the free, and the home of the brave?

On the shore dimly seen through the mists of the deep,
Where the foe's haughty host in dread silence reposes,
What is that which the breeze, o'er the towering steep,
As it fitfully blows, half conceals, half discloses?
Now it catches the gleam of the morning's first beam,
In full glory reflected now shines in the stream,

'Tis the star spangled banner, O! long may it wave
O'er the land of the free and the home of the brave.

And where is that band who so vauntingly swore
That the havoc of war and the battle's confusion,
A home and a country, shall leave us no more?
Their blood has washed out their foul footsteps pollution.
No refuge could save the hireling and slave,
From the terror of flight or the gloom of the grave,

And the star-spangled banner in triumph doth wave,
O'er the Land of the Free, and the Home of the Brave.

O! thus be it ever when freemen shall stand,
Between their lov'd home, and the war's desolation,
Blest with vict'ry and peace, may the Heav'n rescued land,
Praise the Power that hath made and preserv'd us a nation!
Then conquer we must, when our cause it is just,
And this be our motto—"In God is our Trust;"

And the star-spangled Banner in triumph shall wave,
O'er the Land of the Free, and the Home of the Brave.

Inspired by what he saw, Key wrote the poem. When he published it, the title was Defence of Fort M'Henry.

Key's published poem "Defence of Fort M'Henry."

Flag raise at Fort
Mc Henry

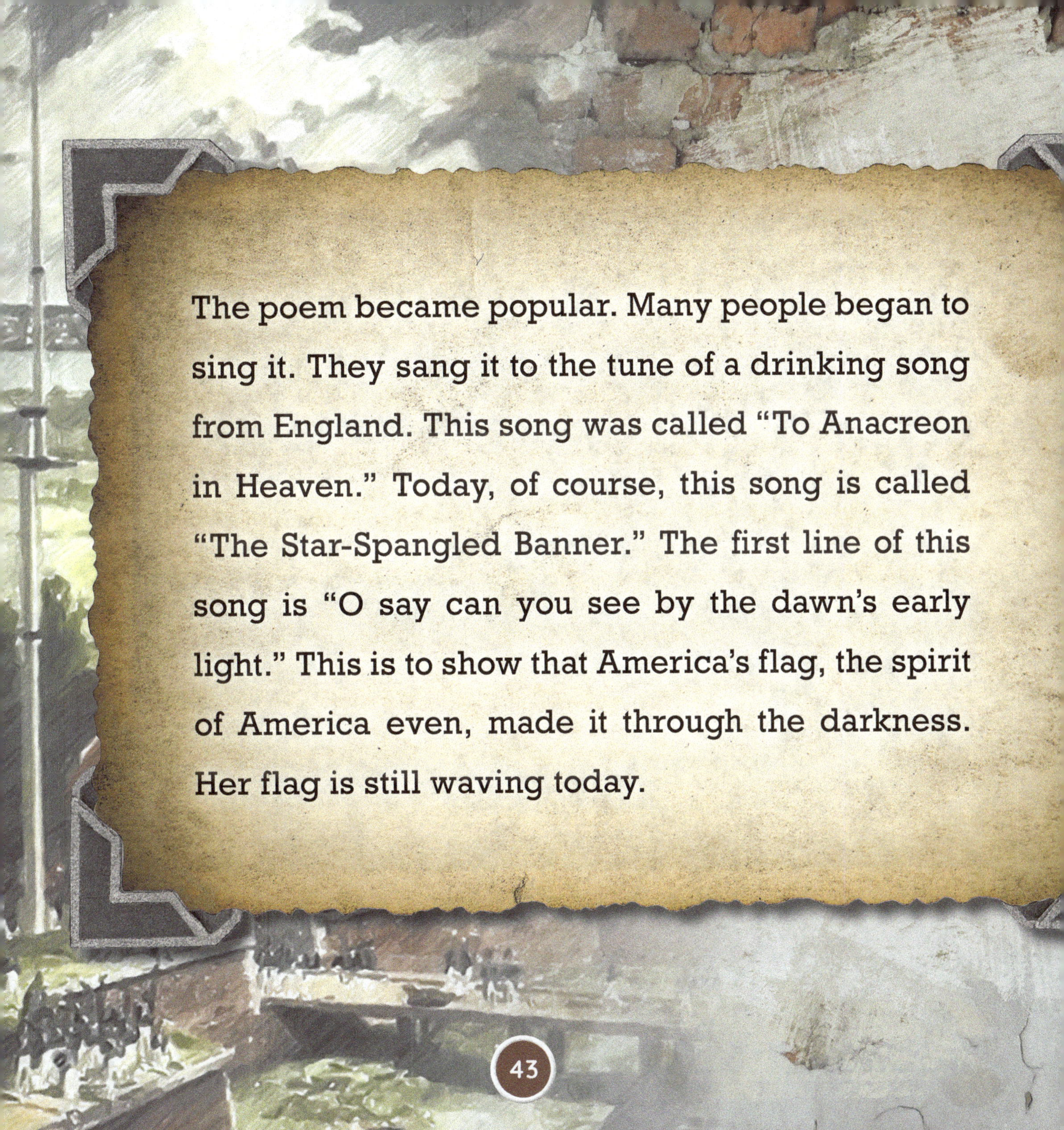

The poem became popular. Many people began to sing it. They sang it to the tune of a drinking song from England. This song was called "To Anacreon in Heaven." Today, of course, this song is called "The Star-Spangled Banner." The first line of this song is "O say can you see by the dawn's early light." This is to show that America's flag, the spirit of America even, made it through the darkness. Her flag is still waving today.

It was chosen to be the official national anthem in 1931. There are four verses in the song. Most people only sing the first verse though. Today, the anthem is sung at parades and ceremonies. It is also sung before sporting events.

The Star-Spangled Banner is sung before sporting events.

People singing the national anthem with respect

When the national anthem is sung, people are expected to stand. This is a sign of respect and love. People should also remove their hats. Some people might even put their hand over their heart. If there is an American flag, people look at it as they sing.

National Anthems From Other Countries

One of the oldest national anthems is "God Save the Queen". It is also called "God Save the King." It depends on who is ruling, a man or a woman. This anthem is for the United Kingdom. This was the anthem for Britain when they had many colonies. As a result, former colonies also know the tune. They might sing different words to it.

2.
O Lord our God arise,
Scatter his enemies,
    And make them fall;
Confound their politics,
Frustrate their knavish tricks,
On him our hopes we fix,
    O save us all.

3.
Thy choicest gifts in store
On *George* be pleas'd to pour,
    Long may he reign;
May he defend our laws,
And ever give us cause,
To say with heart and voice
    God save the king.

In the United States, people might sing "My Country 'Tis of Thee." This song is also just called "America". The first verse goes:

My country, 'tis of thee,

Sweet land of liberty,

Of thee I sing;

Land where my fathers died,

Land of the pilgrims' pride,

From ev'ry mountainside

Let freedom ring!

1. America

(My Country, 'Tis of Thee)

2. My native country, thee,
Land of the noble free,
Thy name I love:
I love thy rocks and rills
Thy woods and templed hills;
My heart with rapture thrills
Like that above.

3. Let music swell the breeze,
And ring from all the trees
Sweet freedom's song:
Let mortal tongues awake;
Let all that breathe partake;
Let rocks their silence break,
The sound prolong.

4. Our fathers' God, to Thee,
Author of liberty,
To Thee we sing:
Long may our land be bright
With freedom's holy light;
Protect us by Thy might,
Great God, our King!

5. We love thine inland seas,
Thy groves and giant trees,
Thy rolling plains;
Thy rivers' mighty sweep,
Thy mystic canyons deep,
Thy mountains wild and steep,
All thy domains.

6. Thy silver Eastern strands,
Thy Golden Gate that stands
Fronting the West;
Thy flowery Southland fair,
Thy North's sweet, crystal air:
O Land beyond compare,
We love thee best!

In Australia, "God Save the Queen" was replaced with "Advance Australia Fair". This happened in 1984.

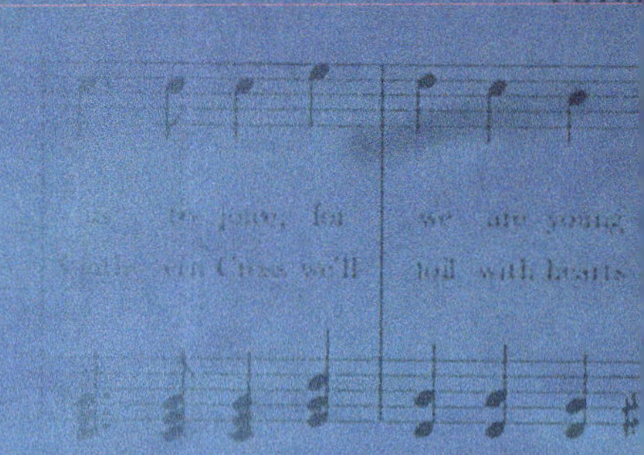

A map of Australia

"La Marseillaise", or the "Song of Marseille", is the national anthem in France. It was written during a war. This is similar to what happened in the United States. For France, the war was the French Revolution.

French Revolution, 1789

THE MARSEILLES HYMN.

Song of the French Revolution.

Ye sons of Freedom, wake to glory!
Hark! hark! what myriads bid you rise!
Your children, wives, and grandsires hoary,
Behold their tears and hear their cries.
Shall hateful tyrants, mischiefs breeding,
With hireling hosts, a ruffian band,
Affright and desolate the land,
While peace and liberty lie bleeding?
To arms! to arms! ye brave!
Th' avenging sword unsheath:
March on! march on! all hearts resolv'd
On victory or death.

Now, now, the dangerous storm is rolling,
Which treacherous kings confederate raise:
The dogs of war, let loose, are howling,
And lo! our fields and cities blaze;
And shall we basely view the ruin,
While lawless force with guilty stride,
Spreads desolation far and wide,
With crimes and blood his hands embruing.
To arms! to arms! ye brave, &c.

In Canada, the national anthem is called "O, Canada". It can be sung in two languages: English and French. This is because Canada has two official languages.

India's national anthem is "Jana-gana-mana". It means "Thou Art the Ruler of All Minds". It was written by a famous poet called Rabindranath Tagore.

Rabindranath
Tagore

53

Changes in politics can cause a national anthem to change. For example, "Deutschland, Deutschland über Alles". This means "Germany, Germany Above All". This was used by the Nazis, who did horrific things.

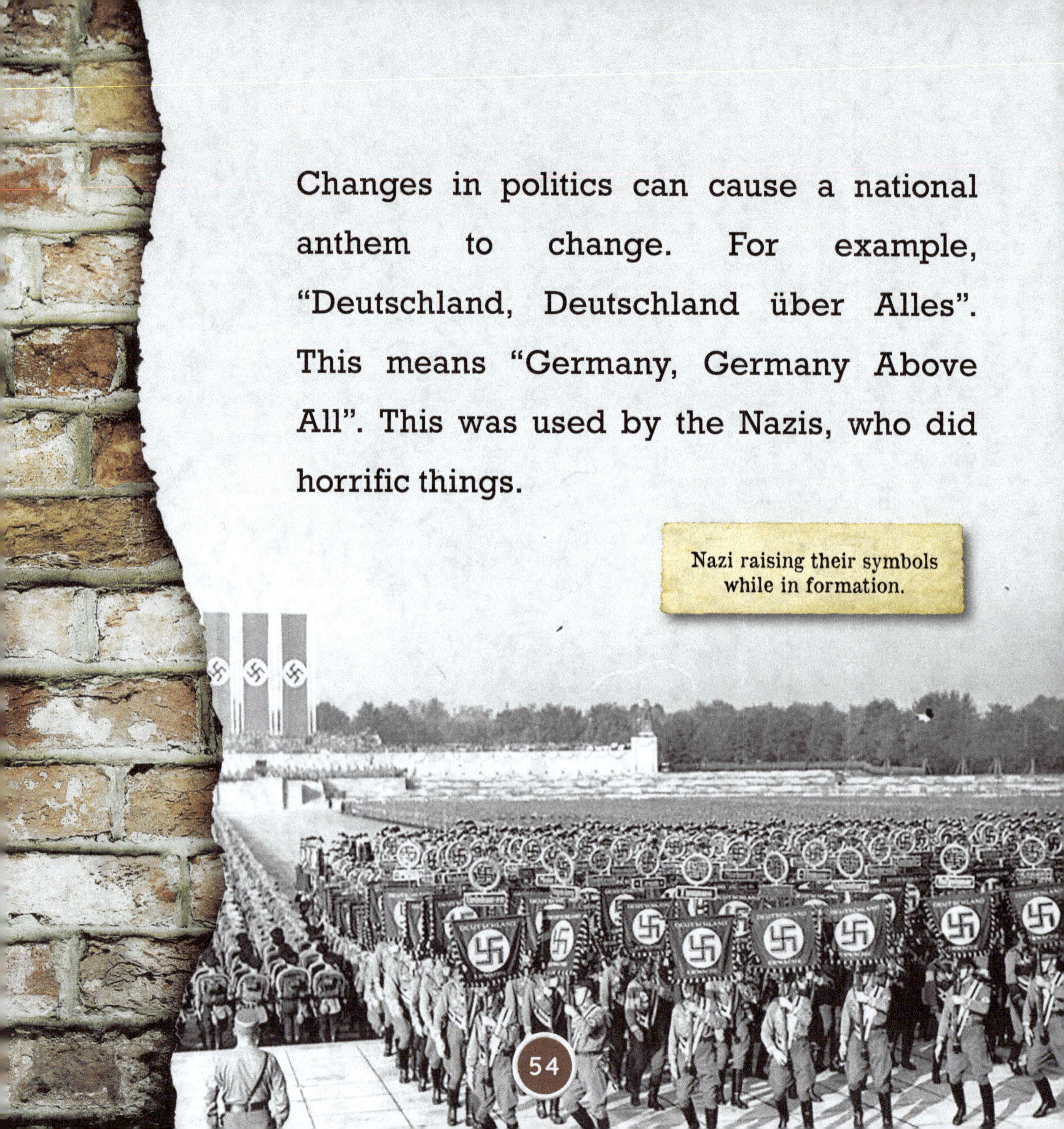

Nazi raising their symbols while in formation.

That is why, after World War II, Germany stopped using the anthem. Today, the national anthem is named "Deutschlandlied". This means "Song of Germany". However, the song still uses the same words.

Germany national anthem "Deutschlandied"

CHAPTER THREE
The Pledge of Allegiance

Allegiance means to be loyal to something. To pledge means to make a promise. The pledge of allegiance is a promise of loyalty to the United States. It shows respect.

A woman pledging allegiance

Many people say the pledge of allegiance at school. They stand, take their hats off, and place their hands on their hearts. Then they look at the flag. They say:

"I pledge allegiance to the flag of the United States of America and to the republic for which it stands, one nation under God, indivisible, with liberty and justice for all."

Students say the pledge of allegiance at school.

60

The pledge was first published in 1892 in a magazine. It was written for young people by Francis Bellamy. Some words in the pledge have changed since then. It was recognized as an official pledge in 1942. The pledge is also said at public ceremonies or large gatherings.

Francis Bellamy

DID YOU KNOW?

The original pledge did not say "under God." This was not added until 1954 under President Eisenhower. It was added in response to the Cold War with Russia. This change upset some people. They did not think that it was right. Not everyone believes there is one God. Others think that the Church and the State should be completely separated.

President Eisenhower, 1959

Social Education 77(4), pp 184–191
©2013 National Council for the Social Studies

"Under God" and the Pledge of Allegiance: Examining a 1954 Sermon and Its Meaning

Eric C. Groce, Tina Heafner, and Elizabeth Bellows

On the first Sunday of February 1954, President Dwight D. Eisenhower and first lady Mamie Eisenhower attended the New York Avenue Presbyterian Church, just down the street from the White House. The sanctuary had hosted several presidents in its history, including John Quincy Adams, Andrew Jackson, and Abraham Lincoln. In honor of Lincoln's birthday, the first couple sat in Lincoln's pew as Rev. Dr. George MacPherson Docherty delivered a stirring sermon advocating that the Pledge of Allegiance include the phrase "under God." Within four months, President Eisenhower had signed the bill into law.

President Eisenhower and Rev. Docherty greet parishioners at the New York Avenue Presbyterian Church in Washington, D.C., on February 7, 1954.

How did this happen and what does it mean? In this article, we explore these issues and provide a lesson plan for examining the topic with a high school social studies class (pp. 188–191). We summarize Rev. Docherty's argument, then offer a lesson that invites students to place his sermon in historical context with the use of a timeline. Students then examine a key passage from the handtyped sermon—a primary historical document—comparing it with other notable quotes of varying points of view.

A Minister's Sermon

Docherty, a graduate of Glasgow University, emigrated from Scotland in 1950 when he was 39 years old. In his sermon titled "A New Birth of Freedom," he recalled a recent afternoon when his children came home from school and recited the Pledge for him.

"I could listen to those noble words as if for the first time," he said. However, he felt something was missing.

The sermon began by noting that the "true strength of America" lies in "the spirit of both military and people—a flaming devotion to the cause of freedom within these borders." Docherty then described the "American Way of Life" with a long series of images and memories: "losing heart and hat on a roller coaster ... setting off firecrackers with your children on the Fourth of July ... school girls wearing jeans and school boys riding enormous push bikes...." He contrasted these images with statements by "a newspaper editor" that Docherty dismissed as platitudes: "It is free and I believe it is freedom to act."

Docherty arrived at "a strange conclusion." There was something missing in this Pledge—the characterizing and definitive factor in the "American Way of Life." He worried that little Muscovites could "repeat a similar pledge to their hammer and sickle flag in Moscow" because Russia also claimed to be a republic that had "overthrown the tyranny of kingship." "Under God," he said, were the "definitive words" missing from the Pledge of Allegiance. The phrase could distinguish our nation's oath of loyalty from the other's.

Docherty supported this by drawing from the work of notable Americans.

Why Patriotism is Important

The United States of America fought for its freedom. They decided everyone had a right to have a say. They should have a government that listens to them.

The United States fought for its freedom.

Everyone should be able to live the way they chose. This means they had freedom of speech and freedom of religion. They could not be punished without a fair trial. There are many other liberties as well.

People have the freedom of speech and religion

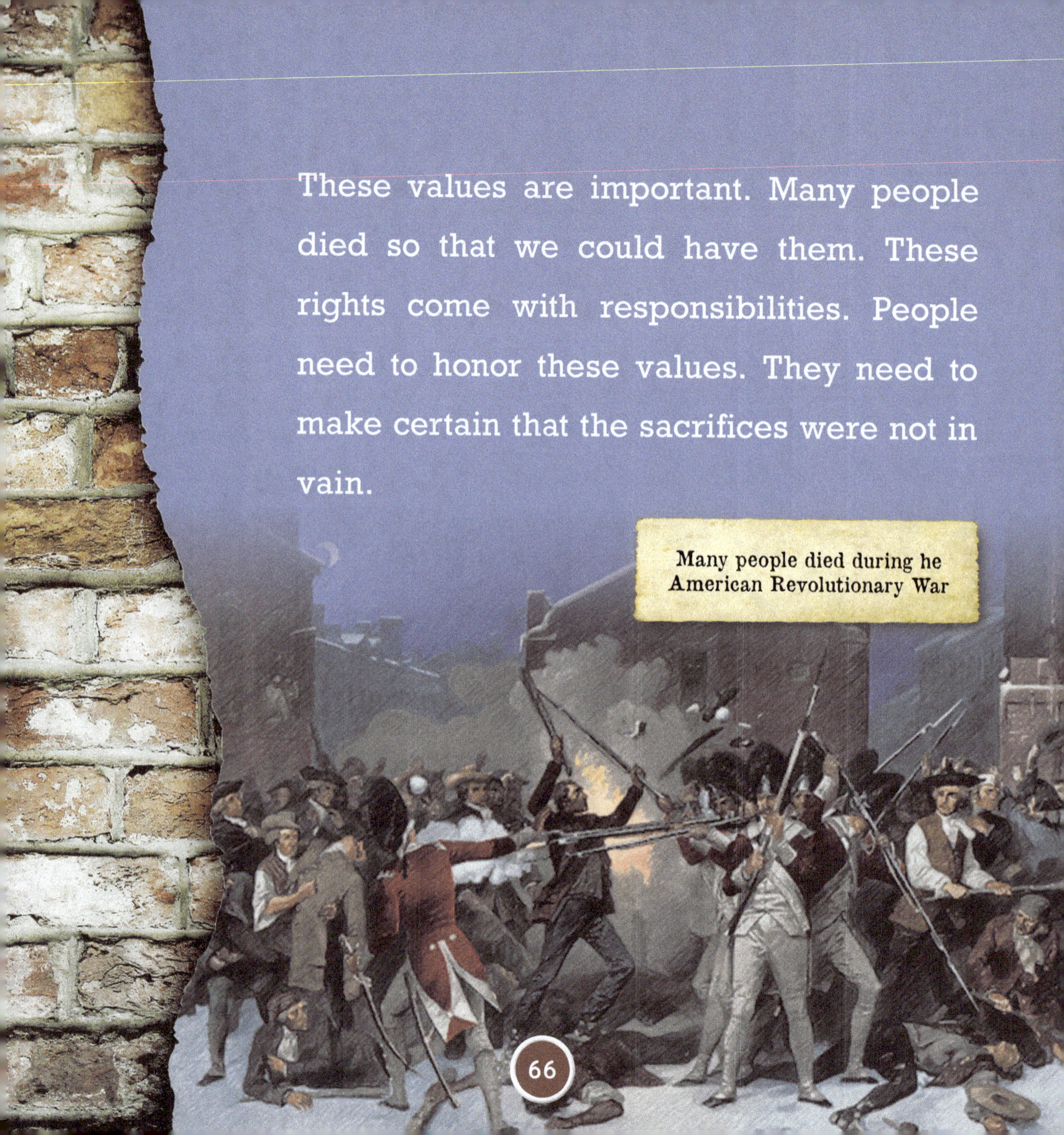

These values are important. Many people died so that we could have them. These rights come with responsibilities. People need to honor these values. They need to make certain that the sacrifices were not in vain.

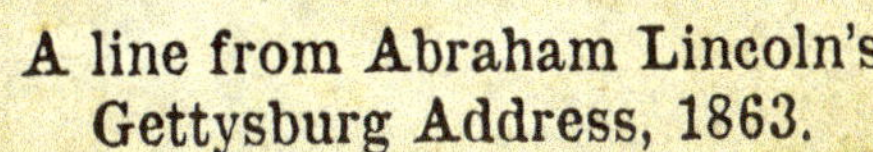

"we here
highly resolve . . .
that government
of the people,
by the people,
for the people,
shall not
perish from
the earth."

—Abraham Lincoln Gettysburg Address 1863

The government "by the people, for the people" cannot work without "the people." This means you! It means that it is your job to be a part of society. It is your job to do your part to make America a great place to live in.

America was founded on the idea of freedom for all people. Many people sacrificed their lives for it. That is why it is important to honor that sacrifice. Patriotism means being loyal to your people and country. It does not mean you have to agree with everything. It means you love your country.

You like what is good, and you want to improve what is not. The American government is one where people can have a say. There are many ways to show the loyalty you have to the United States. You can honor the flag. You can stand and show respect when the anthem is sung. You can say the pledge of allegiance. To learn more about the history of the United States, look for more Baby Professor books!

Visit

www.speedypublishing.com

To view and download free content on your
favorite subject and browse our catalog of new
and exciting books for readers of all ages.